This Book Belongs To:

Given by:

Date of Water Baptism:

My Baptism Story:

AltizerDesigns.com

Library of Congress Control Number: 2024949053

Hardback ISBN: 979-8-9899610-2-3
Paperback ISBN: 979-8-9899610-1-6
e-book ISBN: 979-8-9899610-3-0

Editor: Matthew Brent Altizer

WATER BAPTISM

A GUIDE TO ASSIST CHILDREN AND ADULTS IN UNDERSTANDING BAPTISM AND WHAT IT MEANS TO BE BAPTIZED

Through the Gospel of Jesus Christ

WRITTEN AND ILLUSTRATED BY:

SARAH PACE ALTIZER

Seminole, Florida

FOREWARD

Author Sarah Altizer's new book, "Water Baptism" is a timely book to help our children to understand the necessity of getting baptized. As a senior pastor for over forty years, I want the children of my church to understand not only why they need to be baptized but, what does baptism mean. Sarah's book communicates so well both of these points so that not only kids but, adults can understand the importance of being baptized. This is an excellent book for any church that is hungry to see their people following in the path of Jesus.

Dr. Nick Gough, MTS, D.Min
Senior Pastor, The Branchnc

Sarah Altizer has written an excellent explanation and guide for water baptism. This book beautifully illustrates and describes the journey one takes when choosing to follow Christ through participation in water baptism. The in-depth explanations and biblical sources create an effective and relatable resource for any parent, teacher, or Christian education program. Sarah obviously put lots of prayer, thought, and heart into this endeavor, and it clearly shows. I highly recommend this book for any and all who help young people grow in their faith.

Mark Cooper, MTheo, MDiv.
Senior Pastor, Decatur Foursquare Gospel Church

Sarah Altizer's book on water baptism wonderfully describes in words a pivital truth in scripture. I am amazed at her obedience in following the prompting of the Holy Spirit to write and release a book that explains the beautiful process of water baptism, backed by Scripture, that points us to following the example Jesus so clearly gave us in the gospels, by being baptized himself. It is important that we teach and steward our children's hearts, pointing them to the truth in Scripture. As for me and my house, we will serve the Lord, knowing it is the Lord who defines truth, through his precepts, his Word, the example and teachings of Jesus, empowered by the Holy Spirit. I highly recommend Sarah Altizer's book "Water Baptism" as it is a great way to teach children about the scriptural truth of water baptism.

Rebekah White Williams
Worship leader, Songwriter

DEFINE BAPTISM

WHAT DOES IT MEAN TO BAPTIZE?

Have you ever put a washcloth or sponge in water to get it completely soaked... like dripping wet, no dry parts at all? This is what the word "baptism" means when speaking of water baptism. It literally means to wash, submerge or immerse. In regards to Spirit baptism, which will be discussed in the latter part of the book, it means to be overwhelmed and filled to overflowing by the Holy Spirit.

EVEN JESUS HIMSELF WAS BAPTIZED

Even though Jesus was perfect and did not do anything wrong, He was still baptized by his cousin John in the Jordan River. This was to show Israel that He was the One they had been waiting for, the Messiah. Jesus went all the way under the water and all the way up, and then something amazing happened; the heavens tore open and the Holy Spirit came down like a dove. The voice of God spoke, "This is my beloved Son, in whom I am well pleased."

When you are water baptized, you may not hear the audible voice of God but you will hear others cheering for your big decision.

"This is My beloved Son, with whom I am well pleased."
Matthew 3:17

THE FATHER, SON AND HOLY SPIRIT

ONE GOD IN THREE PERSONS

Of all the things God could have said, He told us that He loves Jesus and He is very pleased with Him. God sent the Holy Spirit, like a dove, not just to touch down and go back up to heaven but to come down and remain with Jesus. God the Father, Jesus the Son and the Holy Spirit intertwined to battle against satan our enemy. Jesus did nothing without the Father's guidance and the Holy Spirit's power.

Read John 1:29-34

Why did John baptize Jesus if Jesus was sinless?

_____

John 1:31

Who came down and remained on Jesus?

_____

John 1:32

IMMERSION | GOING UNDER WATER

Because we are following in the steps of Jesus when we become a Christian, full immersion is what we practice too. The thought of having to go completely under water can be intimidating, but it is very special when you know why you are doing it. Let's go to the beginning of the story and find out.

The Gospel | From Fall to Redemption

In the beginning, God spoke life into existence... **CREATION**

"Let Us make mankind in Our image, according to Our likeness; and let them rule over the fish of the sea and over the birds of the sky and over the livestock and over all the earth, and over every crawling thing that crawls on the earth." Genesis 1:26

THE FALL OF HUMANS

THE FIRST MAN AND WOMAN

Adam and Eve had two very important jobs: First, to be friends with God and second, to take care of Eden. Their world was perfect and was a great place to live. Life was easy for Adam and Eve. The people and animals all got along with each other. There was not any pain and most importantly, Adam and Eve could talk with their God any time they wanted to. He was their friend.

Tree of Life

Tree of the knowledge of good and evil

SIN ENTERS THE WORLD

It is kind of hard for us to understand how perfect the world was compared to where we live now. Something sad happened that ruined this perfect world; through a lie from satan and disobedience to God, SIN entered the world. God's only rule was not to eat from the tree of the knowledge of good and evil. Satan talked them into breaking this rule by lying about what God ACTUALLY said. He twisted God's words and Eve believed satan over God. She ate from that tree and gave some to Adam to eat also.

WHAT IS SIN?

We sin any time we make choices that go against God's Word. Sin is disobeying God and His commandments. We were created to know and walk with God. We were created in His image!

What sin examples can you think of?

Read God's Commandments | Deuteronomy 5:6-21

Who is the only Perfect One?

Read 1 Peter 2:22, Hebrews 4:15, 2 Corinthians 5:21

SIN AND SACRIFICE

OUR GOD IS PERFECT AND ALL KNOWING

Sin makes our hearts dirty. The problem with being sinful is that God is HOLY, so we cannot be around Him when we sin. God loves us, so this made him very sad. God had to make Adam and Eve leave the garden of Eden because of their sin. Even at the fall, God in His love and mercy kicked them out of the garden, because He didn't want them to eat from the tree of life, which would cause them to live eternally with sin. Their friendship with Him changed. This separation was difficult on people and on God. All choices, good and bad have consequences, and the consequence of sin is separation from God and also death.

But...God was working BEHIND THE SCENES to make another way to reconcile us to Himself again. Even at this point of kicking them out, God made His plan for Jesus to crush satan and draw people back to Himself.

God made the first sacrifice to cover their sin by covering their bodies with the skin of an animal. In order to continue to talk to God, their sin had to be covered. For a time, He would forgive the peoples sins by having them continue to make a sacrifice through taking the life of an animal. The life is in the blood, and the blood would make attonement for their sins. This was a temporary solution.

A NEW BETTER WAY

Sin separates us from our loving God. The people had to atone for their sins by sacrificing a pure animal, whose blood would provide forgiveness and reconciliation to their creator. They had to do this on a regular basis, because they would sin again and have to make another sacrifice. The shedding of blood of a pure animal to forgive sins was the old covenant practice. For a long time this was the way it had to be, so people could talk to God and He could answer their prayers. But, God had a better plan, a new covenant, and He planned it from the moment Adam and Eve sinned.

This better plan is the gospel, meaning good news. This would be the new covenant (agreement) between Him and us. The new agreement would allow us to come bodly to God through His Son Jesus Christ. He didn't keep it a secret but He told prophets all throughout history; we can read about it in the Old Testament. The plan was to come to earth and become the perfect sacrifice to cleanse people of their sins once and for all. His blood was better than pure animals, because He is God, the perfect spotless lamb. He would do for us what we could not do for ourselves.

The Bible, which is God's Word, is all about God's plan and love for mankind. The Old Testament is all about creation and prophets telling about the coming of Jesus in the future and real people who walked and talked with God. The New Testament is telling about Jesus being born, walking among us, and Him dying on the cross for our sins. It continues to teach how He beat sin and death by being raised from the dead, walking alive for 40 days and then returning to heaven with the Father. Jesus is the final permanent sacrifice for the salvation of mankind.

Even though men wrote the words in the Bible, why can we trust it?

Read 2 Timothy 3:16-17

OLD TESTAMENT

ALL ABOUT JESUS

Prophets Fortell
Looking Forward
Temporary Sacrifice
Animals Cover Sin

JUSTIFIED BY FAITH

NEW TESTAMENT

ALL ABOUT JESUS

Apostles Testify
Looking Back
Permanent Sacrifice
Jesus Takes Away Sin

JUSTIFIED BY FAITH

It Is Finished

GOD AMONG US

JESUS IS SON OF GOD AND SON OF MAN

Jesus is God, therefore perfect and HOLY. He was also born of a woman, which means He has a human body. He came down to learn our language and make friends (and enemies), but He was/is still God.

God the Holy Spirit impregnated the virgin Mary. To be a virgin means that she had not been with a man, so her pregnancy was miraculous. He was born in a manger in Bethlehem and grew up just like you and me, growing in wisdom. He would preach in the Temple throughout His life, but He would not start His full ministry until after He was baptized by John in the Jordan River. He was fully God because He was born of the Holy Spirit, and He was fully human because He was born of a woman.

What did the angel of the Lord tell Joseph in his dream?
What does His name Emmanuel mean?

Read Matthew 1:18-25

JESUS UNDERSTANDS

Jesus suffered as we suffer, so He can empathize with what we are going through. This is God's lovingkindness and mercy to walk as we walk, in order to relate to us; He is our friend. He was tempted as we are, but He did not sin. Jesus did nothing apart from the Father and did not use His own powers, becoming a servant in the likeness of man. We too can ask and receive as Jesus did. He shows us the life He wants us to walk, relying on God the Father. This is not to say we walk a completely sinless life but because Jesus has now broken the power that sin had over us, we can walk in power and truth with the help of the Holy Spirit. Outwardly we are fading away, but inwardly we are being renewed on a daily basis, meaning we will grow in truth and wisdom in our spirit.

Read: Romans 6
Deuteronomy 30:11-16
2 Corinthians 4

JESUS SACRIFICES HIS LIFE

Jesus was killed on the CROSS. The consequence of sin is death. Satan thought he had won, but Jesus was without sin, so He came back to life. While He was on the cross, He took the world's sins upon Himself, making the ultimate final sacrifice. There would no longer be need for temporary animal sacrifice. Jesus' blood was better than the animal sacrifice, because it would take away the sins of mankind (not simply cover their sins). Jesus became the final permanent sacrifice for the salvation of mankind.

So now the new covenant (agreement) between God and man is:

THE GOSPEL
If you confess with your mouth Jesus as Lord, and believe in your heart that God raised Him from the dead, you will be saved; for with the heart a person believes, resulting in righteousness, and with the mouth he confesses, resulting in salvation. Romans 10:9-10

Why did God become fully human?

_____

Read Hebrews 2:14-18

What do we become in Christ as a result of His sacrifice?

_____

Read 2 Corinthians 5:21

JESUS LIVES

HE WALKED AMONG THE PEOPLE

After Jesus had risen from the dead, He spent 40 days walking and talking with over 500 people including Mary, James, Peter, the apostles, and many other friends. After the 40 days, He had to go back to heaven, but He didn't do this to leave everyone alone. However, He said it was good for him to go so another could come.

THE PROMISE OF THE HOLY SPIRIT

After Jesus left and went up into the clouds to heaven, He would send the Holy Spirit who is the presence of God, to indwell the believers. He came down in a mighty way on the day of Pentecost. The Holy Spirit gave them the ability to speak in other languages and to prophesy in Jesus' name. You can read about it in chapter 2 of the book of Acts. The Holy Spirit would give the friends of Jesus power to live Holy lives and obey everything Jesus said. Even today the Holy Spirit lives inside everyone who makes the choice to follow Jesus and gives us the power to obey and do great things for God.

Read: Acts 2

BORN OF WATER AND OF THE SPIRIT

At water baptism you are declaring Jesus as your Savior (publicly), but at Spirit baptism you are declaring Jesus as your LORD over all of your life. Water baptism is of repentance, which is John's baptism (John the baptist). Jesus' baptism is of the Holy Spirit and fire. It is the Holy Spirit not only indwelling you (happens at salvation), but remaining and filling you to overflowing. You are inviting the Holy Spirit to purify you and make you clean, just as gold is refined in the fire. As you walk with Him in you, He wants to burn all that is unholy in your life. He also gives you a boldness to share the gospel with others, and power to heal in His name.

And it shall be in the Last Days,' God says, 'That I will pour out My Spirit on all mankind; and your sons and your daughters will prophesy, and your young men will see visions, and your old men will have dreams; and even on my male and female servants I will pour out My Spirit in those days, and they will prophesy. Acts 2:17-28

16

BECOMING A BELIEVER

SALVATION

"I believe in you Jesus"

WATER BAPTISM

"I repent of my sins"

BAPTISM BY SPIRIT AND FIRE

"Purify me and make me Holy"

WHY WATER BAPTISM

Just before Jesus went up into the clouds after walking amongst the people for 40 days, He tells His disciples to teach all nations, and to baptize them in the name of the Father and of the Son and of the Holy Spirit. This final command is called the Great Commission; It's like the final pep talk. It must have been important as it's His last huddle with His closest followers. And so, baptism is a significant command in that pep talk. Therefore when we are baptized, we are being obedient to Christ's command.

Being Obedient to Jesus' command under the authority He was given by the Father, signifies our surrender to Him. Surrender is an act of obedience, which simply means to trust in God's ways as higher and better than our own and to lean on Him for direction (action) and understanding (discernment). If we truly want to live our lives in worship to God, then you will be obedient to His commands. When you love someone, you naturally want to please them.

What did Jesus' obedience do for all humans?

___

Read Romans 5:18-21

A SYMBOL OF YOUR CONFESSION

Peter compares our baptism to the water that flooded the earth in the days of Noah saving 8 people. Water baptism is a symbol of your confession in Jesus Christ that saves you too! It's not as if it's to clean dirt from your body but the pledge of a clear conscience toward God. Jesus being sinless and righteous, died for me who is sinful and unrighteous. Water baptism is a confession of repentance.

By what means do we gain a good conscience toward God?

_____

Read 1 Peter 3:18-22

The flood cleansed sin from the earth. Water baptism is a symbol of confession that sin is being cleansed from our lives.

WATER BAPTISM IS SIMILAR TO A WEDDING CEREMONY

When a man and a woman join in marriage, the wedding day is a symbol of their public confession of love and commitment to their spouse in front of all of their loved ones. Before the big day, the couple has already declared their commitment to each other privately. However, something amazing happens when they publicly declare their faithfulness and exchange rings in front of others; the two become one flesh. Paul calls this a great mystery in the book of Ephesians. In the same way, your water baptism is a pledge to Jesus for the rest of your life. Also, as the two become one flesh at the wedding ceremony, you will be putting on Christ at your baptism ceremony. In the same way, this spiritual transformation is a mystery, in that we all become one in Christ Jesus.

Read: Ephesians 5:31-32

IT IS A BAPTISM OF REPENTANCE

When God shows you your sins, it's not just a sorrowful moment but a moment of truth. You will see sin in your life that you didn't even know was sin! But the cool thing is, the Holy Spirit will teach you what is right and also empower you to walk in truth. Water baptism is a physical experience representing a spiritual occurance of your admitting to your sin and being renewed and cleansed from all unrighteousness. Ask God to show you your heart and the ways in which you are not pleasing to Him and repent. You will receive peace in repentance as you rely on God continually after, turning from your sin. He will show you what is right and wrong and He will place a desire in you to obey Him. It is by the mercy of God that we are led to repentance in water baptism.

What does John say about water baptism?

_____

Read Matthew 3:11

What attribute of God the Father leads us into repentance?

_____

Read Romans 2:4

JESUS WASHES YOUR SINS AWAY

During your baptism think about it like this, as you go under the water, the dirt (sin) goes down with you. As you come up, your sin and disobedience is washed away in the water. Jesus washes your sins away as you have asked Him to. It is by faith and your experience will be personal and spiritual.

A SYMBOL OF THE CROSS

Being baptized into Jesus means that we are also baptized into His death with Him. So this means that we are buried with Him. Obviously we don't physically die during water baptism, but our dead unrighteous old self dies with Him. Consequently, being dead we are free from sin. Our spirit that is made alive as Christ is alive, is how we truly live a new life. This spiritual transformation from death to life is done by the wondrous works of God.

By being baptized into his death, how should we walk?

_____

Read Romans 6:1-8

What does it mean to be crucified with Christ?

_____

Read Galatians 2:20 and Colossians 2:12-14

Buried with Christ

23

A SYMBOL OF THE RESURRECTION

If you have been buried with Christ going under the water, what do you think will happen being raised from the water?

Resurrection!

You are raised with Christ to your new life. Christ has already been raised from the dead and cannot die again; death has no hold over Him. You are now dead to sin, but alive to God, through Jesus Christ.

Once you are raised with Christ, what do you set your heart upon?

_____

Read Colossians 3:1-4

Being raised with Christ, what no longer has a hold over you?

_____

Read Romans 6:8-12

Raised with Christ

IT IS BY FAITH

BAPTISM DOES NOT SAVE YOU

Water baptism does not save you from eternal hell. The LORD tells us that we are saved by simply receiving the gift that God gave us. If you believe in your heart and confess with your mouth that Jesus is the Son of God who died on the cross for your sins and came back to life, then you will be saved. When you accept Jesus as your Savior, you are saved from the consequences of sin, which is separatation from God (hell). This is the gospel, which means good news. Therefore, by His grace, salvation is a free gift by the workings of God, which is based on FAITH, and it is by the LORD's kindness that leads us into repentance and to faith in Him. This free gift is not by our doing but based solely on the works of Jesus.

BAPTISM IS A PUBLIC DECLARATION

At water baptism, it is a public ceremony of death to your old self and resurrection to your new life with Jesus. Think of it like a funeral for a physical death; the person has already died, but the funeral is just a celebration of that persons life, declaring their death to friends and family. At first your salvation is somewhat of a secret until your public declaration at your baptism ceremony.

GRACE AND JUSTIFICATION

Through one man's disobedience (Adam), sin entered the world. Also, through one man's obedience (Jesus Christ), grace and justification abound to many! By the grace of God you have been justified through faith in Jesus. To be justified means Jesus has taken your sins away before the Father. When the Father looks upon you, He now sees the righteousness of Christ and no longer a sinner. God's grace is a free gift!

Further explain what it means to be justified.

Read Romans 5:12-21

AFTER WATER BAPTISM

LET US LOOK AT JESUS AS OUR EXAMPLE

After Jesus was baptized in the Jordan River by John, the Holy Spirit came down on Jesus and remained. After the water baptism, the Holy Spirit immediately led Jesus into the wilderness. Jesus fasted (did not eat or drink) for 40 days and 40 nights. At the mountain top, satan would meet him and tempt him 3 times. Each time satan would entice Jesus to either gratify His flesh or operate outside of the Father's will. With each temptation, Jesus would overcome satan by using the Word of God (Scripture), which IS truth. God the Father gave us a real life example for us to imitate through His son Jesus. Jesus was fully God, but also fully human, meaning that He came in the likeness of a man, as a servant, in order to not only redeem mankind but to show us the life we are able to live by relying fully on the Father.

What are the three temptations that satan presented to Jesus?

_____

Read Matthew 4:1-11

WHAT ABOUT ME?

Don't be surprised in the coming weeks or months that you may come across temptations. When you do, imitate Christ by using truth (the Word of God) to demolish any lies (temptations) that the enemy may throw at you. That means you should continue to learn the Scriptures so you may be armed in the coming days and years.

Remember, we are given the ability to walk a life pleasing to God through Christ's justification and the Holy Spirits direction. However, do not fall into pride which many easily do. We have been saved by grace through the works of God and not by our own doing.

Read Ephesians 6:10-20, which explains what the armor of God is and why we need to put it on.

STAYING HUMBLE

All humans have sinned and all are in need of the saving grace of God. If anyone thinks he has not sinned, then the truth of Christ is not in them. That being said, when you do make a mistake, you can go quickly and with confidence to God's throne of grace and ask for forgiveness. He promises to cleanse us from all unrighteousness. The biggest responsibility going forward is walking a humble life alongside God. Remember that Jesus sent you His helper, the Holy Spirit whom you may ask anything and He has promised to lead us into truth.

Staying humble means to not think too highly or too lowly of ourselves, but to rest in our reliance on Jesus. Let Jesus teach you, for His ways are not burdensome.

How can we stay humble like David?

_____

Read Psalms 25

Why do we need to be steadfast in faith and humility?

_____

Read 1 Peter 5:5-11

A NEW PERSON IN CHRIST

When you believed in the work of Jesus Christ, you became a new person. The old life is gone and now a new life has begun. You no longer see things from a human point of view but now have heaven's perspective. The Holy Spirit will give you the ability to walk in love, joy, peace, patience, kindness, goodness, faith, meekness and self-control, as you walk close to Jesus; for these are the fruits of the spirit. As you remain in close relationship with the Lord, you will bear much fruit!

THE NARROW GATE

JESUS IS THE NARROW GATE

The life ahead of you is a beautiful blessed life, but it will not come easy. There is still pain, suffering and troubles in this fallen, broken world, but the Holy Spirit will guide you every step of the way. You simply have to ask for His help. He will answer you through a small quiet voice and will always align with God's Word.

The narrow way that leads to life is your personal journey with the Lord and the narrow gate you will enter into eternity is through Jesus. The Holy Spirit will be your guide.

Take comfort and read John 14

TRIALS AND HARDSHIPS

This narrow path will come with trials and hardships, but do not be discouraged. The LORD will use these difficult situations to do a mighty work in your heart building you up to be a mighty warrior. Remember your armor from reading Ephesians? Your battle is not against flesh and blood but against spiritual dark forces in this world. That is why Jesus tells us to pray continuously.

When facing difficult situations, it is important to listen to others with care and consideration and to listen more than you are speaking. When you do speak, consider your words carefully, prayerfully and with intentionality. Do not become angry easily, but if you do come into anger, which itself is not sin, do not allow your anger to cause you to sin. God will give you the wisdom you need for each situation as you seek Him and ask His advice and for help. Oftentimes, certain conflicts require spiritual weapons (prayer and fasting), because they cannot be reasoned with human logic.

Why should we be confident when hardships come upon us?

Read James 1:1-8

BORN FOR A PURPOSE

These earthly bodies will continue to fade over time, but our spirits will continually grow day by day. We will gain new heavenly bodies when this current body fails us. For Jesus is preparing a place in heaven for us! But in the meantime, you were born in this generation, at this present time, for a very important purpose.

Once we are reconciled to God, our purpose is to help others be reconciled to God. Through Christ, who never sinned, the LORD reconciled the world back to Himself by no longer counting their sins against them by way of repentance (confession and forgiveness.) This gift of reconciliation is based on God's work and not our own, so we cannot take credit for it. Jesus gives us the ability to do good works and plead with the world to be reconciled to God. This light you now have will shine in dark places and people will be drawn to know Him through your representation of Jesus.

You are ambassadors for Christ!

When Jesus called Matthew, why did the religious leaders complain? What was Jesus' response?

Read Luke 5:27-32

33

THE SIMPLE LIFE GOD COMMANDS

The life that God asks us to live is not too far off or hard. The LORD wants us to learn His ways so we may walk in life and blessings. Jesus told us that all of the law and the prophets hang on the first two commandments. The top commandment is that we are to love God with all of our heart, soul and mind. The second commandment is that we are to love our neighbor as we love ourselves.

Now go and walk an honest life with Christ!

The simple life God commands is to
Seek Justice, Love Mercy & Walk Humbly with your God
Read Micah 6:6-8

THE AUTHOR'S BAPTISM

It was March 2000 and I was a student at Virginia Tech. I decided to join a friend of mine in Panama City Beach Florida with Campus Crusades for Christ on Spring Break. It was on this trip where I would sit quietly with my first Bible and ask Jesus to be my Savior. Shortly after this, I woud leave Virginia Tech to attend a local Bible college so that I could truly learn and understand what the Word of God says and means.

The first year of my attendance at Life East Bible College, Nick Gough was the pastor at the school's church. He is an incredible man of God and became a significant teacher and mentor to me during that season of my early 20's. It was in my first year at the school in 2001 when I would get water baptized.

I remember Pastor Nick asking me a question about my faith and I professed my love and desire to know and walk with Christ in front of the church. He then baptized me in the name of the Father, the Son and the Holy Spirit, pulling me completely under the water and then coming up from the water. The spiritual experience I had in that moment was exactly as the Word of God declares and what I have written in this book about baptism. I spiritually felt my old self die (buried) and the new self being risen to life with Christ. I have never felt anything like it before and I have never experienced anything like it since.

God's heart for mankind is for all men, women and children to know Him and love Him and to come into the knowledge of truth. This is not a salvation of religion or a man's doctrine but a salvation by the only One True Living God, the Creator of life, who sent His Son Jesus in the flesh to rescue His children from their sins and to give them living water and eternal life.

I would love to hear about YOUR baptism experience! Email me at altizersarah@gmail.com.

With Love in Christ,
SARAH PACE ALTIZER

www.ingramcontent.com/pod-product-compliance
Lightning Source LLC
Chambersburg PA
CBHW041128120626
46547CB00019B/2906